LOST AND FOUND

written by
Anne W. Phillips

illustrated by
Regan Dunnick

HARCOURT BRACE & COMPANY
Orlando Atlanta Austin Boston San Francisco Chicago Dallas New York
Toronto London

All of these sheep have lost Little Bo Peep.
Who will help them find her?

"Not me," said the cat.
"I'm chasing a rat."

"Not me," said the pig.
"I must eat and grow big."

"Not me," said the duck.
The hen just said, "Cluck!"

The sheep looked around.
You know who they found!